Medieval Knights

by Grace Hansen

Abdo Kids
THE MIDDLE AGES
Kids

Abdo Kids Jumbo is an Imprint of Abdo Kids
abdobooks.com

abdobooks.com

Published by Abdo Kids, a division of ABDO, P.O. Box 398166, Minneapolis, Minnesota 55439.

Printed in the United States of America, North Mankato, Minnesota.

052025

092025

THIS BOOK CONTAINS RECYCLED MATERIALS

Photo Credits: AdobeStock, Alamy, Getty Images, Look and Learn, Shutterstock

Production Contributors: Teddy Borth, Jennie Forsberg, Grace Hansen
Design Contributors: Candice Keimig, Pakou Moua

Library of Congress Control Number: 2024947605

Publisher's Cataloging-in-Publication Data

Names: Hansen, Grace, author.

Title: Medieval knights / by Grace Hansen

Description: Minneapolis, Minnesota : Abdo Kids, 2026 | Series: The Middle Ages | Includes online resources and index.

Identifiers: ISBN 9798384905318 (lib. bdg.) | ISBN 9798384906018 (ebook) | ISBN 9798384906360 (Read-to-me ebook)

Subjects: LCSH: Knights and knighthood--Juvenile literature. | Knights and knighthood--Europe--History--Juvenile literature. | Middle Ages--Juvenile literature. | Medieval history--Juvenile literature. | Dark Ages--Juvenile literature.

Classification: DDC 940.1--dc23

Table of Contents

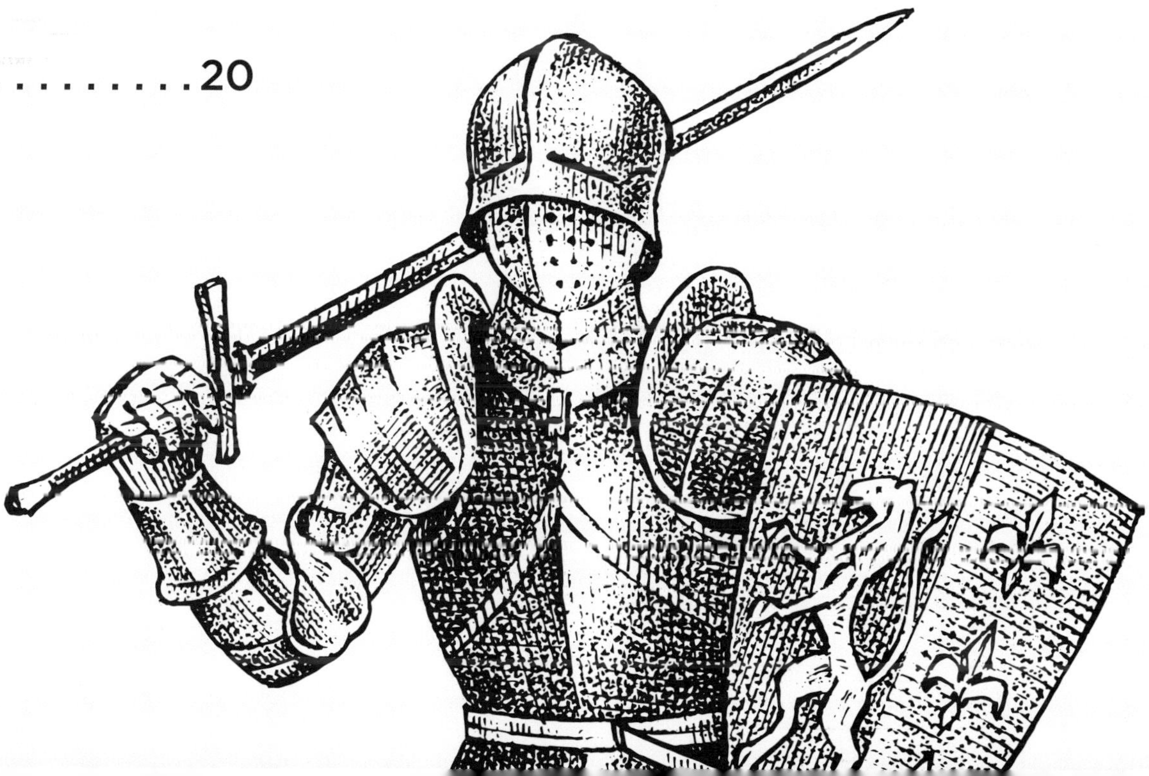

The Middle Ages

The Middle Ages, or medieval period, was a time in European history. It lasted from about 500 to 1500 CE. Knights lived during this time.

Europe
Asia
Africa

Respected Soldiers

Knights were soldiers. They served in the armies of powerful men. Knights lived in castles or large **manors** owned by their **lord**.

Knights lived by a code called **chivalry**. This code said that knights had to be **loyal** and fair. They also had to protect people. Knights were good and brave men.

Becoming a Knight

Knights were trained from childhood. When a boy was around 7 years old, he could become a page. Pages learned to handle horses, hunt, and use fake weapons.

At around age 14, a page could become a squire. Squires had more responsibilities. They began to use real weapons. They also helped knights.

When a squire turned 18, he was usually ready to become a knight. Squires became knights in a dubbing **ceremony**.

Clothing

In battle, knights wore chain mail, plated armor, and a helm. These items protected them from arrows and swords.

Helm
Chain mail
Plated armor

In daily life, knights were very **fashionable**. They wore outfits made of nice cloth such as silk, wool, or linen. Their clothing was often colorful to show their high **status**.

Jousting

Knights always had to practice their skills. They often joined jousting tournaments. In these events, knights charged at one another on horseback. The goal was to knock the other knight off their horse.

Famous Knights Today

Great Britain still honors people by knighting them for their achievements. Men receive the title of Sir. Women receive the title of Dame.

Sir Lewis Hamilton

Formula One driver

Notable Achievements

- Multiple F1 championships
- Holds over 100 F1 records
- Activist

Sir Elton John

Musician

Notable Songs

- "Rocket Man"
- "Tiny Dancer"
- "Goodbye Yellow Brick Road"

Sir Patrick Stewart

Actor

Notable Roles

- Captain Jean-Luc Picard in *Star Trek*
- Charles Xavier in *X-Men*

Dame Emma Thompson

Actor

Notable Roles

- Mrs. Potts in *Beauty and the Beast* (2017)
- Sybill Trelawney in the *Harry Potter* films

Glossary

ceremony – an official act or series of acts done in a certain way to honor a special occasion.

chivalry – the system, ways, and customs of knighthood. Knights were expected to show chivalry through strength, bravery, and more.

fashionable – dressing according to the current trend.

lord – a title for a nobleman.

loyal – showing faithfulness to someone or something.

manor – a large piece of land and its main house or mansion.

status – a person's position or rank compared with others.

Index